Harbour Island, Bahamas

Tourism, Travel Guide

Author
David Mills.

SONITTEC PUBLISHING. All rights reserved. No part of this publication may be reproduced, distributed, or transmitted in any form or by any means, including photocopying, recording, or other electronic or mechanical methods, without the prior written permission of the publisher, except in the case of brief quotations embodied in critical reviews and certain other noncommercial uses permitted by copyright law. For permission requests, write to the publisher, addressed "Attention: Permissions Coordinator," at the address below.

Copyright © 2019 Sonittec Publishing
All Rights Reserved

First Printed: 2019.

Publisher:
SONITTEC LTD
College House, 2nd Floor
17 King Edwards Road,
Ruislip
London
HA4 7AE

Table of Content

SUMMARY 1
ABOUT HARBOUR ISLAND, BAHAMAS 4
TOURISM 7
   THINGS TO SEE IN HARBOUR ISLAND 12
   THINGS TO DO IN HARBOUR ISLAND 18
   ACTIVITIES ON HARBOUR ISLAND 24
      Bikes & Mopeds.. 30
      Diving 33
      Nightlife 35
      Shopping 38
      Best Restaurants in Harbour Island 43
      Best Nightlife in Harbour Island 51
      Snorkeling 53
   ATTRACTIONS IN HARBOUR ISLAND 57
   HARBOUR ISLAND ACCOMODATION... 61
      Hotels 67
      Villa Rentals 73
   BEST HOTELS FOR SHORT VACATION OR BUSINESS TRIP 85
   TRANSPORTATION 88
      Air Travel 92
      Ferries 98
      Rental Cars 101
      Sailing & Boating 104
   IMPORTANT INFORMATION 108
      My Harbour Island Personal Experience 111

Harbour Island, Bahamas

Summary

The world is a book and those who do not travel read only one page.

It is indeed very unfortunate that some people feel traveling is a sheer waste of time, energy and money. Some also find traveling an extremely boring activity. Nevertheless, a good majority of people across the world prefer traveling, rather than staying inside the confined spaces of their homes. They love to explore new places, meet new people, and see things that they would not find in their homelands. It is this very popular attitude that has made tourism, one of the most profitable, commercial sectors in the world.

People travel for various reasons. Some travel for work, others for fun, and some for finding mental peace. Though every person may have his/her own reason to go on a journey, it is essential to note that traveling, in itself, has some inherent advantages. For one, for some days getting away from everyday routine is a pleasant change. It not only refreshes one's body, but also mind and soul. Traveling to a distant place and doing exciting things that are not thought of otherwise, can rejuvenate a person, who then returns home, ready to take on new and more difficult challenges in life and work. It makes a person forget his worries, problems, frustrations, and fears, albeit for some time. It gives him a chance to think wisely and constructively. Traveling also helps to heal; it can mend a broken heart.

For many people, traveling is a way to attain knowledge, and perhaps, a quest to find answers to their questions. For this, many people prefer to go to faraway and isolated places. For believers, it is a search for God and to gain higher knowledge; for others, it is a search for inner peace. They might or might not find what they are looking for, but such an experience certainly enriches their lives

David Mills

About Harbour Island, Bahamas

Affectionately called "Briland" by it's residents, Harbour Island is one of the oldest and most charming of settlements in the Bahamas. Once the capital of the Bahamas and the second largest city to Nassau in the early 1900s, the current population is estimated around 1,500. The island is located approximately 200 miles from Miami, 60 miles from Nassau and 2 miles east of Eleuthera.

On Harbour Island, you'll see 18th century buildings restored in a Bahamian brigadoon setting. This three-mile long half-mile wide island is world-renowned for its pink sand beaches, quaint shops and extraordinary cuisine. Harbor Island's offerings range from five star dining to a variety of "conch shacks" that line the Harbour as well as a vibrant nightlife.

Eleuthera was originally occupied by Lucayan Indians. In 1648, Captain William Sayles set sail from Bermuda with a group of English puritans looking to escape religious oppression. They named the beautiful island they found "Eleuthera" which is the Greek word for "freedom". Dunmore Town, named after Lord Dunmore, Governor from 1786-1797, is the main and only town on Harbour Island and one of the oldest settlements in the Bahamas. A small quaint village featuring New England architecture, Dunmore was known for its ship building and sugar refinement in the late 1800s. Making rum was particularly popular during Prohibition.

While Harbour Island has a very colorful history, the island is best known for its pale pink sand beaches some three plus miles long and 100 feet wide considered one of the very best pink sand beaches in the world. On Harbour Island, there's something for everyone; including fine cuisine at family style restaurants, world class scuba diving, deep sea fishing, fly fishing for bone fish, surf fishing, horseback riding on the beach, shelling, day trips to Eleuthera and Spanish Wells, and shopping for souvenirs from the sidewalk vendors in Dunmore Town

Tourism

Harbour Island in the Bahamas is quietly becoming the crown jewel of the Caribbean. A small island a few miles off of Eleuthera may only be 3 ½ miles long by a half mile wide (at its widest) with fewer than 2,000 residents, but it is jammed packed full of beautiful beaches, pastel painted cottages with picket fences, quaint boutique hotels and restaurants that rival the best found in other culinary hot spots such as St. Barts and Anguilla.

Like many other best islands to visit in the Caribbean, this one is hard to get to. Most people who travel on commercial flights fly in to North Eleuthera's airport via Miami, Atlanta and Ft.

Lauderdale, while others opt for Nassau followed by a short flight. There are also charter services, such as Air Flight Charters, a reliable service that operates out of Ft. Lauderdale (you can book individual seats if a charter is already scheduled or book an entire plane, depending on the size of your party). If you fly into North Eleuthera, you will then go by taxi for the short ride to the dock ($5 per person) and then you will hop on a motor boat for the short trip to Harbour Island (also $5 per person). Upon arriving at Harbour Island there are several taxis that will be waiting to take you to your hotel (also for $5 per person).

Harbour Island is a tropical oasis with miles and miles of seemingly endless pink sand beaches. Most people rent golf carts to get around the island, and there are several companies that rent them including Michael's Cycles(which also rents bicycles, boats and kayaks) and Johnson's Rentals.

It is possible to rent golf carts that offer 2, 4 or 6 seats and you can arrange for the cart to be waiting at your hotel or at the dock when you arrive by boat (if you know the way to your hotel).

Most of the boutique hotels have reserved spots on a beach for their patrons and offer chaise lounges and umbrellas. There are also spots where it is possible to rent a chaise lounge and umbrella by the day. The sea is warm---even on a recent cool day in early January, the water temperature was warmer than the air temperature and was very comfortable for taking a swim.

The top boutique hotels on the island are The Ocean View Club and The Dunmore. There are others worth checking out, including the Pink Sand Resort (25 guest cottages), Coral Sands Hotel and The Rock House (10 rooms). The Ocean View, which is bohemian chic offers twelve rooms, some of which are stand-alone. All offer ocean views, as the name of the property implies. The Dunmore is a bit more sophisticated with 10 acres of manicured grounds, a tennis court and a heated oceanfront swimming pool. It offers 16 newly renovated private cottages including a few 2 to 4 bedroom oceanfront homes.

What Harbour Island is perhaps best known for, however, is its excellent restaurants and plethora of outdoor activities. Some of the best restaurants on the island include The Ocean View Club, The Dunmore, The Rock House, The Landing, Da Vine Wine and Sushi (a combination wine shop and sushi restaurant that is owned and operated by a former Nobu chef) and the beachside Sip Sip (only open for lunch).

Reservations are recommended at most restaurants and some, such as The Dunmore, require a credit card to hold a reservation and will charge a $50 per person cancellation fee if you don't show up or if you cancel within 24 hours. Harbour Island is not an inexpensive place to visit and most of the restaurants tend to be on the expensive side (main courses for dinner are often priced as high as $48), but the food is almost always excellent. Locals and frequent visitors swear by the family-owned Queen Conch for its famous conch salad and soup for lunch and Arthur's Bakery for homemade doughnuts and fresh raisin bread.

The island's famous pink sand beaches are among the best found anywhere in the Caribbean. The beaches are expansive and there are always plenty of chaise lounges to go around, unlike other island destinations. There are plenty of private boats that are available for charter should you want to go snorkeling, fishing or have a beach picnic on a small nearby island.

Things to See in Harbour Island

Dunmore Town, located on the island's harbor side, was named for the 18th-century royal governor of The Bahamas who had his summer home here. You can walk around the narrow, virtually car-free lanes in less than 20 minutes, or stroll slowly to savor the sight of the old gingerbread cottages lining the waterfront. Draped with orange, purple, and pink bougainvillea, white picket fences enclose wooden houses painted pastel blue, green, and lilac. Wind chimes tinkle in front of shuttered windows while coconut palms and wispy casuarina pines shade grassy yards.

Americans and Canadians own some of these houses, which have whimsical names, such as Up Yonder and Beside the Point, instead of house numbers. One of the oldest, Loyalist Cottage, was built in 1797. It survives from the days when the original settlers, loyal to the British Crown, left the American colonies after the Revolutionary War.

The porches along the harbor make for prime sunset-watching. Lucky for you, some porches aren't connected to private homes. The terrace at the Harbour Lounge is an idyllic perch. Just across the road from Loyalist Cottage, you can browse through straw goods, T-shirts, and fruits and vegetables at vendor stalls.

On Sundays, dressed-up residents socialize in clusters outside churches before and after services. Two of the first churches in The Bahamas are in Dunmore Town, still going strong: St. John's, the country's oldest Anglican church, established in 1768, and Wesley Methodist Church, built in 1846.

Spend some time wandering the streets -- some hilly, some flat -- away from the heart of town. You can see roosters doing their jerky marches through front yards and horses grazing in small fields. In this locals' area, you'll come across some unassuming but perfectly good Bahamian restaurants, bars, and nightclubs.

Its hallmark are pink beaches - an amazing natural phenomenon, that gives a miniature island a huge popularity. The explanation for this amazing natural phenomenon is quite simple. Mollusks Foraminifera inhabit the coastal waters of the island. Their shells have a rich pink colour. They dash against the coral reef in a storm or waves and afterwards, they mix with white sand. The beaches look just spectacular.

In addition to unusual natural attractions, there are also noteworthy historical sites on hte island, the study of which will diversify your rest. Dunmore Town is the capital of the island and its only city. Travellers are recommended to start acquaintance with the historical heritage of the island with a walk along its central Bay Street. It is worth noting, that the city owes its name to Lord Danmoor, the Governor of the Bahamas, and the main historical symbol of the capital is the Danmore cottage. The construction is very impressive. Next to it, is a memorial dedicated to outstanding political figures

There is an old sugar mill nearby, built more than one and a half centuries ago. For many years, active mining of sugar cane was conducted here. It is noteworthy, that the surviving mill is completely ready for use. A very unusual attraction is a Fig Tree Park, which will excite not only lovers of nature, but also tourists who have interest in history. For many years it has provided a venue for the most important social events. It was in the park, among the mighty trees, that the most important political and social issues had been solved, solemn events and national holidays had been held.

A pleasant place for hiking will be an old shipyard district, near which are the ruins of an old fort. The construction of the fortress has been held under the leadership of the legendary pirate Charles Wayne. To see the ruins of the once mighty structure will be interesting to everyone. The coastal zone is rich in beautiful grottoes and caves. In the 18th century one of the largest caves was converted into a prison. Nowadays, it is one of the most visited sightseeing objects. You will find many curious walking routes on the territory of the miniature island. Amateurs of sightseeing and active entertainment never be bored.

To the service of guests of Abaco, there is a fantastic choice of comfortable areas suitable for beach recreation. Great Abaco Island is the location of Tahiti Beach. This is an internationally famous beach with white sand and lush tropical flora. Rows of tall palm trees grow near the water, so vacationers do not need to have a sun umbrella as they can always hide under the shade of trees. Water is crystal clear in this area, so it is perfectly suitable for snorkeling and admiring colorful fish.

Numerous travelers are in love with Treasure Cay Beach and are delighted with its calm and peaceful atmosphere. This coastal area is a big one, so it is never crowded. At the beach, there is a popular restaurant with a rich selection of food. Lush tropical forests near the beach make this area even more attractive. Upscale travelers often choose Marsh Harbour Island as their vacation destination. The island has many luxurious hotels that are built directly in the middle of tropical forests. Each of these hotels has a comfortable private beach. It is an ideal destination for a trouble-free vacation and all kinds of water sports. In recent years, several modern diving centers have appeared on the island

Things to Do in Harbour Island

One of the oldest settlements in The Bahamas, founded before the United States was a nation, Harbour Island lies off Eleuthera's northern end, some 322km (200 miles) from Miami. It is 5km (3 miles) long and 1km (2/3 mile) wide. The media have hailed this pink-sand island as the new St. Barts, a reference to how chic it has become. These days, beware: If you're jogging along the beach, you might trip over a movie star.

Affectionately called by its original name, "Briland," Harbour Island is studded with good resorts. The spectacular Pink Sands Beach runs the whole length of the eastern side of the island and is protected from the ocean breakers by an outlying coral reef, which makes for some of the country's safest swimming. Except for unseasonably cold days, you can swim and enjoy watersports here year-round. The climate averages 72°F (22°C) in winter, 77°F (25°C) in spring and fall, and 82°F (28°C) in summer. Occasionally, evenings are cool, with a low of about 64°F (18°C) from November to February.

To the amazement of even the island's most reliable repeat visitors, its clientele has gotten almost exponentially richer and more famous since the turn of the millennium. There's a building boom of ultra-upscale villas and a migration into the island by some staggeringly wealthy billionaires who have included Ron Perlman (CEO of Revlon) and India Hicks (a relative of England's royal family and former fashion model). Colin Farrell, Sylvester Stallone, and Sarah Ferguson, the Duchess of York, along with various titled aristocrats from the old houses of Europe, make discreet but strategic appearances throughout the winter months. This new influx of the mega-wealthy has.

Tampa's Lowry Park Zoo

Tampa's Lowry Park Zoo has a lot to offer all ages. This zoo is located at 1101 West Sligh Avenue in Tampa, Florida. It is home to over 1,500 animals. You can see bears and tigers or visit the lively chimpanzees. This zoo is home to many different birds too. If you want to see endangered manatees, this zoo is the place to go. You can enjoy walking around and seeing all sorts of animals. If you get hungry, there are many different dining options. There are also nice gift shops located around the zoo. The cost of admission is $24.95 for adults and $19.95 for children under 11. Children under three get in free. Tampa's Lowry Park Zoo is an adventure waiting to happen. Your entire family will have an unforgettable time touring this fun attraction.

Florida Aquarium

A trip to the Florida Aquarium while visiting Tampa Florida is a great way to spend several hours out of the sun. One can enter the penquin's world, and enjoy the cute artic birds. Swimming with fish and diving with sharks are also available options. The aquariam has a two acre outdoor water park that allows children a fun way to cool off. Parents can relax while the children enjoy so many activities in a safe and contained area. Seeing dolphins in the wild is a must on dolphin cruises. The tickets are an affordable day of fun for everyone. Adult admission is under twenty dollars, and children eleven and under are under sixteen dollars. There is a senior citizen discount available. One can even enjoy a meal or special event surrounded by walls of beautiful fish. Weddings, corporate events, and private parties are also available.

Big Cat Rescue

Big Cat Rescue, BCR, is an animal sanctuary located at 12802 Easy Street in Tampa, Fla. The sanctuary is home to over 100 large cats, include tigers, lion, bobcats and cougars. Many of the animals were rescued from abuse or were abandoned by their owners. Big Cat Rescue is instrumental in educating the public about the plight of cats and seeks to end their abuse, both in the wild and in captivity. Guided tours are available to the public. All tours of the sanctuary are educational in nature. Photos and video are allowed but smoking, cell phones and umbrellas are not. As a 501-c-3 organization, BCR has the highest Charity Navigator rating, with 100 percent of donations used for supporting the animals and stopping big cat abuse. Tours are offered to adults and children over the age of 10 for $29 per person. Feeding tours and night tours are available for $55 per person.

Busch Gardens

Busch Gardens in Tampa Bay, Florida is located on 10165 North McKinley Drive and is home to beautiful wild animals that have been rescued, saved, rehabilitated, loved and cared for daily. It is a park where you can visit, learn, and interact with the animals and zookeepers, while watching animal shows and enjoying some thrilling amusement park rides that provide experiences like you have never had before. Some of the best animal attractions at Busch Gardens to visit are the Animal Care Center, the Bird Gardens, the Cheetah Run, the Edge of Africa, Jambo Junction and Jungala. Some of the best shows to watch while you are at this lovely park is A is for Africa and Critter Castaways. If you want to ride some thrilling rides, the best ones are the Cheetah Hunt, Wild Surge, Sand Serpent and the Congo River Rapids. If you are an explorer, you should consider taking one of the many safari tours offered at Bush Gardens such as the Sunset Safari. The price for a ticket to get into Busch Gardens for a day is $75.00 for adults and $67.00 for children.

Activities on Harbour Island

Known as the "Nantucket of the Caribbean," Harbour Island has a unique feel to it with its New England style buildings set to the backdrop of a tropical island. Like the diversity of the landscape, the typical type of tourist attracted to this destination ranges from the top one percent of earners to beach-goers traveling on a budget. While the perfect pink sand beaches are generally what attracts tourists, there are many activities to consider as you plan your getaway.

It is probably not hard to imagine that waterports rank at the top of the list of favored activities. Scuba diving, fishing, and sailing are how many tourists spend the majority of their time on the island. What you may not know is that this is one of the top dining destinations in the Bahamas, and while you probably do not consider eating the type of activity that you would put so much thought into, on Harbour Island it is essential that you do.

Bike and Scooter Rental

Harbour Island is one of those places where eveyone uses golf carts to get around. Join in on the fun and do some exploring like a local. Alternatively, bikes and scooters are also a good option.

If you are considering seeing the sights at a slower pace, you will encounter 6 places that can help you. To read more about this specific topic, read from Bike and Mopeds page concerning options for renting a bike or scooter.

Diving

Harbour Island is one of the most varied diving destinations in the Caribbean. Offering a mix of reefs, caves, and canyons, you can find any kind of terrain off the island. With this variety also comes an abundance of marine life that make for a great experience.

You'll find a couple of dive services and a small number of interesting dive sites in the area. Go to Diving page in this book dedicated to scuba diving in this area if you're interested in learning more specifics.

Sailing and Boating

The following table enables you to get more information about firms that can help you get out on the water.

Boating Opportunities On Harbour Island

Name	Type	Phone	Location	Island
Valentines	Boating and Day-Sailing Provider	(242) 333-2080	Dunmore Town, Central Harbour Island	Harbour Island

If you're interested in learning about local marinas and charter options read from boating and sailing page in this book.

Shopping

If you're going to be traveling with some avid shoppers they might enjoy visiting a few of the 11 retail shops in the area. For information concerning opportunities for shopping on Harbour Island, read from shopping page in this book.

Sightseeing

Yet another good way to spend some of your vacation is exploring the area's sights and natural beauty. Sights of interest to visitors include a few historic sites and various other attractions of interest to travelers. For more information about this topic, read on attraction page in this book concerning area sightseeing opportunities and attractions.

Snorkeling

If exploring an underwater world sounds appealing you're in luck -- you'll have plenty of chances to do so within easy reach of Harbour Island. To see our complete page about local snorkeling opportunities, see from snorkeling page in this book.

Spas

Relaxing for a few hours in a spa might be one of the most enjoyable parts of your entire vacation. If a spa visit sounds like fun, you will be happy to discover there's one in the area.

Tennis

If you'd like to play some tennis during your visit you might want to make your reservations at a hotel with a tennis court. You can choose between two different properties in the area that offer tennis.

The table below may help with your planning. At a glance, you'll see the number of tennis courts on-site, whether lighting is available for evening play, and a few other details. Click on each name to learn more about the property.

Accommodations With Tennis On Harbour Island

Property	Location	Tennis Courts	Lit Courts	Tennis Pro
Coral Sands Hotel	Dunmore Town, Central Harbour Island	2		

| Pink Sands Resort | Dunmore Town, Central Harbour Island | 2 | | |

For instance, Coral Sands Hotel is located directly on the beach, where you can go and relax between games.

Bikes & Mopeds

Renting a Bike or Scooter on Harbour Island
Although golf carts are the main mode of transportation on Harbour Island, there is another option for tourists to consider, renting a bicycle. Although few people even consider, it is a great way to remain outdoors as you travel from one destination to the next, and even allowing you access to sites you may not have otherwise had the opportunity to see.

If you are considering riding in the open air, there are a variety of different businesses that can help.

If you'd like to go riding, you might want to contact Michael's Cycles. Michael's Cycles is dedicated to providing you with the most friendly rental service and quality rentals. With over 20 years of experience on Harbour Island, they are a trusted service for all your rental needs. They are located in Dunmore Town, in central Harbour Island.

Another good option is Dunmore Rentals. For more than 30 years, Dunmore Rentals has been offering golf cart rentals to visitors of Harbour Island, particularly in Dunmore Town. Set on the corner of Bay and Church Streets, they are conveniently located near the ferry docks. You can reach them at (242) 333-2372.

A third option is Johnson's Rentals. Featuring the newest selection of golf cart rentals on the island,

Johnson's Rentals offer a lot of perks, like drop off and pick up, and the option of two, four, and six-seater carts. located in Dunmore Town, in central Harbour Island. They're

Take a moment to read the table just below to learn more about area rental agencies.

BIKE AND MOPED RENTAL ON HARBOUR ISLAND		
Name	Phone	Location
Dunmore Rentals	(242) 333-2372	Dunmore Town, Central Harbour Island
Johnson's Rentals	(242) 333-2376	Dunmore Town, Central Harbour Island
Major's Golf Cart Rentals	(242) 470-5065	Dunmore Town, Central Harbour Island
Michael's Cycles	(242) 464-0994	Dunmore Town, Central Harbour Island
Ross Garage Cart Rentals	(242) 333-2122	Dunmore Town, Central Harbour Island

Diving

Scuba Diving Near Harbour Island

The underwater landscape of Harbour Island abounds with mysterious caves and canyons, while the coral reef is alive with colorful fish, sponges, and algae. There simply is no bad location for a dive in this area. If you've got an interest in the sport of scuba diving, you can sign up for a day certification course at the very least and get under the surface of the sea immediately.

You'll find one dive service, a dive shop, and a small number of dive sites in the area.

Dive Operators and Shops

The dive shop available are provided right below.

Dive Shops Near Harbour Island

Name	Type	Phone	Location	Island
Valentines Dive Center	Dive Shop//12577	(242) 333-	Dunmore Town, Central	Harbour Island

		2080	Harbour Island	

If you'd like to go diving, you might want to check with Valentines Diving. Valentine's offers many fun activities for a variety of customers, including daily dives, snorkeling, private charters, and multilevel certification courses. Rental equipment is also available at Valentines Dive Center for those who would like to kayak, paddle board, or go on a fishing charter. They are located in Dunmore Town, in central Harbour Island.

The chart below shows a few details regarding the only dive service in the area that we are aware of.

Dive Operators Near Harbour Island				
Name	Type	Phone	Location	Island
Valentines Diving	Dive Service//12576	(242) 333-2080	Dunmore Town, Central Harbour	Harbour Island

Harbour Island, Bahamas

Island

Dive Sites

A few key facts concerning some of the area's major dive sites are provided right below.

Dive Sites Near Harbour Island

Name	Quality	Experience	Max Depth	Latitude	Longitude
Devil's Backbone	--	--	--	25.5606181338	-76.6973562241
Devil's Backbone	Good	--	36.1	25.5770333333	-76.6869
Glass Window Bridge	Good	Open Water / CMAS *	62.3	25.4381666667	-76.6036

Nightlife

Nightlife on Harbour Island

The word you might use to describe the nightlife scene on Harbour Island is quirky. Tourists typically don't visit the island to party, but somehow find themselves looking at a clock reading 4:00 a.m. After a night of drinking and dancing at a local bar turned club with live music, locals, and a homegrown feel that makes everyone feel welcome.

You'll find a fair number of bars and nightlife venues on Harbour Island.

If you're ready to experience some local nightlife, you might want to consider Gusty's Bar. It is found within Dunmore Town, in central Harbour Island. Although the bar is always on the busy side, when the DJ comes out at 10:00 p.m. each night, that is when the party really gets started and the sand-floor dance floor is filled with the middle-aged singles crowd that wants to dance and drink the night away.

Another good option is JJ's Night Club. A small no-frills spot to watch the game while you grab a drink, this is the spot to be if you want to experience life like a local. They can be reached at (242) 333-2431.

The table below lists some key facts regarding 5 venues for after-hours relaxation.

Nightlife On Harbour Island

Name	Phone	Location
Charlie's Bar	(242) 333-3039	Dunmore Town, Central Harbour Island
Gusty's Bar	(242) 333-2165	Dunmore Town, Central Harbour Island
JJ's Night Club	(242) 333-2431	Dunmore Town, Central Harbour Island
Seagrapes Harbour	(242) 333-	Dunmore Town, Central

Island	2439	Harbour Island
Vic Hum Club	(242) 333-2161	Dunmore Town, Central Harbour Island

Shopping

Shopping on Harbour Island

The Out Islands of the Bahamas are not necessarily known for their shopping opportunities, but Harbour Island has a nice, charming collection of shops selling the most luxurious items available in the region. If you're looking for unique but high quality products, this is where you'll find them.

Gifts and Souvenirs

If you enjoy shopping for souvenirs or gifts you should think about visiting Calico Trading Co, which is located in Dunmore Town, in central Harbour Island. Calico Trading Co pulls its exotic style from South American designers while also carrying edgy European designers that are fabulous for men, women and children. They also sell beach wear, gifts and toys. If you're looking to call before making reservations, you can do so at (866) 333-3826.

The chart below has some details concerning 3 gift and souvenir shops on Harbour Island.

Gifts And Souvenirs On Harbour Island

Name	Type	Phone	Location
Calico Trading Co	Gift and Souvenir Shops	(866) 333-3826	Dunmore Town, Central Harbour Island
Dilly Dally	Gifts, Souvenirs, and Handicrafts	(242) 333-3109	Dunmore Town, Central Harbour Island
Straw Market Harbour Island	Gifts, Souvenirs, and Handicrafts	--	Dunmore Town, Central Harbour Island

Specialty Shops

One of the area's more popular specialty retailers is Valentines Dive Center. They are found in Dunmore Town, in central Harbour Island. Along with PADI certification courses, {% link_to 1708298 %} offers daily scuba diving trips to multiple locations around the island, from reefs to wrecks. Guests can sign up for snorkeling, boat trips and kayaking as well. To contact them, call (242) 333-2080.

Another good option is The Princess Street Gallery, which is located within a mile to the north of Valentines Dive Center. Featuring an elegant selection of some of the country's more famous works which depict local culture, the Princess Street Gallery is known as one of the most high quality galleries in the Bahamas. They can be found on Princess Street.

Be sure to look at the following table for a list of specialty shops serving Harbour Island.

Specialty Shops On Harbour Island

Name	Type	Phone	Location
The Princess Street Gallery	Art Gallery	(242) 333-2788	Dunmore Town, Central Harbour Island
Valentines Dive Center	Dive Shop	(242) 333-2080	Dunmore Town, Central Harbour Island

Clothing and Apparel

Interested in shopping for clothing? Consider dropping by Sugar Mill -- which is located in Dunmore Town, in central Harbour Island. They have sunglasses, tunics, hats, handbags, scarfs, sandals, jewelry and more! If you want to know more, call them at (242) 333-3558.

The chart just below provides you with more details regarding the 3 apparel shops on Harbour Island.

Clothing And Apparel On Harbour Island		
Name	Phone	Location
Briland's Androsia	(242) 333-2342	Dunmore Town, Central Harbour Island
Miss Mae's	(242) 333-2002	Dunmore Town, Central Harbour Island
Sugar Mill	(242) 333-3558	Dunmore Town, Central Harbour Island

Food and Grocery

Check out this table to learn more.

Food And Grocery Stores On Harbour Island			
Name	Type	Phone	Location
Johnsons Grocery Dunmore Street	Grocery Store	(242) 333-2279	Dunmore Town, Central Harbour Island

Patricia's Fruits and Vegetables	Fruit and Vegetable Market	(242) 333-2289	Dunmore Town, Central Harbour Island
Pigly Wigly Store	Grocery Store	333-2120	Dunmore Town
Sybil's Bakery	Bakery	(242) 333-3011	Dunmore Town, Central Harbour Island

Best Restaurants in Harbour Island

The main feature of Harbour Island's restaurants is there are plenty to choose from and they offer some of the finest food in the Bahamas. The wide variety of restaurants in such close proximity is virtually unmatched on any other Bahamian out island.

Menus range from fine cuisine to local Bahamian fare. Dress codes are usually quite casual with a few instances of semi-formal. Each restaurant has their own unique presentation of Bahamian atmosphere with many offering unforgettable views of the island and its surroundings.

This is only a partial listing of the restaurants you will find on Harbour Island. Finding the other restaurants on this small island is very easy to do - just ask around. You can find the location for many of these restaurants on our map of Harbour Island. It's even more enjoyable and rewarding to spend a few hours touring the island on a golf cart and seeing them firsthand. Ask to look at their menus when stopping by. Some post their daily specials on chalk boards at their entrance.

It is recommended to call ahead to find out what their serving times are and to make dinner reservations in advance.

All listed telephone numbers are area code 242.

Harbour Island, Bahamas

<u>Valentines Boat House Restaurant</u> - You will have your choice of savoring your meals on our open-air deck on the water or dine in air conditioned comfort and enjoy of our dramatic waterfront view. From our kitchens come bistro favorites and elegant seafood fare. Come evening, you never know who you'll be rubbing elbows with as our bar draws a jet-set crowd of island hoppers. 333-2142

<u>Runaway Hill Inn</u> - Runaway Hill Inn restaurant is oceanfront dining that fuses fresh local cuisine with imported ingredients offering nouveau Caribbean exotic to ensure you a fantastic dining experience. Casual elegance defines the restaurant said by many to be the best that Harbour Island has to offer. Reservations recommended but walk-ins are welcome pending availability. 333-2150

<u>Acqua Pazza</u> - At Harbour Island Marina. Mediterranean flair to Bahamian fish and seafood plus Italian dishes. 333-3240

<u>Coral Sands</u> - At Coral Sands Resort. Overlooks lagoon pool with the ocean as backdrop. 333-2350

<u>The Dunmore</u> - Dine inside the cozy, breeze-filled dining room or in the open air on the breathtaking ocean view terrace. 333-2200

<u>The Landing</u> - historical boutique hotel serves an excellent contemporary menu based on local produce and freshly caught seafood. 333-2707

<u>Pink Sands</u> - The cuisine at Pink Sands' casual Blue Bar and more formal Garden Terrace reflect Caribbean flavors and local ingredients. 333-2030

<u>Rock House</u> - Upscale menu in a casual yet elegant setting perched on the bluff in Dunmore Town overlooking the bay. 333-2053

Sip Sip - Serves lunch only. Expensive but excellent food. Gorgeous view of the ocean. 333-3316

Sunset Bar and Grill - Breakfast, lunch and dinner, all in a casual, tropical atmosphere. 333-2325

Sit-down Native Restaurants – Day and Evening

Ma Ruby's - On Colebrook Street. Home of "Cheeseburger in Paradise." 333-2161

Angela's Starfish - On north Dunmore. 333-2253

Local Restaurants on Harbour Island

Native, affordable and casual - some are lunch only.

Queen Conch - Bay Street north of the dock. Conch salad and more! Lunch AND dinner now. 333-3811

The Shack - Coral building at end Government dock; a few seats or carry it out. 333-2542

Tiki Hut - Colebrooke Street. Lunch and dinner. 699-5992

Sugar Rush - Pitt Street. Breakfast sandwiches, lunch and baked goods.   333-2451

Avery's - On Colebrook Street. Serves Bahamian dishes daily except Tuesdays. Open all day and evenings except Tuesdays. 333-3126

Wade's Take-Away - North Bay Street near Fishermen's Dock. Recommended native food.

Harry O's - North Bay Street near Fishermen's Dock. Recommended native food. 333-3478

Brian's BBQ - Dunmore Street. 333-3129

Tropic Hut - Also known as the "pizza place" on Dunmore Street.
333-3700

Breakfast and Lunch on Harbour Island

Arthur's Bakery - On Dunmore Street. 333-2285

Bahamas Coffee Roasters - On Dunmore Street. 242-470-8015

Dunmore Deli - On King Street. 333-2644

Sybil's Bakery - Duke & Dunmore Streets. 333-3011

Coffee & Beverages

Cocoa Coffeehouse - Bay Street next to Valentine's Resort. 333-1323

Night Life and Night Clubs

Gusty's - Coconut Grove Street. 333-2165

Daddy D's - Dunmore Street on top of Tropic Hut & across from Arthur's Bakery.

If you don't want to dress up for lunch, head for Seaview Takeaway, at the foot of the ferry dock (tel. 242/333-2542). Here you can feast on all that good stuff: pig's feet, sheep-tongue souse, and, most definitely, cracked conch. Everything tastes better with peas 'n' rice. Daily specials range from $3 to $9. It's open Monday through Saturday from 8am to 5pm.

Another casual drop-in spot for both visitors and locals is Arthur's Bakery & Cafe, Dunmore Street (tel. 242/333-2285; www.myharbourisland.com/bakery.htm), owned by Robert Arthur, the screenwriter for *M*A*S*H*. Artists, writers, media people, and what Arthur calls "international lollygaggers" hang out here. There are only a few tables, and they fill up quickly with those catching up on local gossip. Arthur's Trinidadian wife, Anna, bakes the island's best Key lime tart and is also praised for her croissants and banana bread. At lunch, drop in for fresh salads and sandwiches. Many guests come here to use the Internet, too.

Ma Ruby's Conch Burger -- If you'd like to sample some real local fare, head to Ma Ruby's, on Colebrook Street (tel. 242/333-2161). Some dyed-in-the-wool locals claim you'll get the best down-home cooking in Harbour Island if Ma Ruby (the cook and owner) is in the kitchen herself. She's been stewing chicken, baking grouper, and serving hearty meals in a trellised courtyard for a long time, and she's amassed a lot of devoted fans. Her conch burger is certainly worthy of an award. The place is also known for its cheeseburgers, which the manager says were ranked as one of the world's 10 best by "Mr. Cheeseburger in Paradise" himself, Jimmy Buffett. Prices range from $6 to $15 for the a la carte menu; a four-course fixed-price Bahamian dinner costs $24 to $40. The restaurant is open daily from 9:30am to midnight

Best Nightlife in Harbour Island

Unpretentious Gusty's, on Coconut Grove Avenue (tel. 242/333-2165), boasts sweeping sea and sunset views and a clientele that's drawn from every strata, top to bottom, of Harbour Island's complicated sociology. Inside is a sand-covered floor, while the outdoor veranda is sometimes the scene of fashion shows for local dressmakers. Live music is featured every night. Gusty's opens nightly at 9:30pm and then goes on rocking virtually until dawn.

Sea Grapes, on Colebrook Street (no phone), another favorite of locals, is where you can boogie down to the sounds of disco or catch a live band. Expect to be jostled and crowded on a Saturday night because everyone on the island comes here for a wild Bahamian hoedown.

Vic-Hum Club, on Barracks Street (tel. 242/333-2161), established in 1955, is the quintessential

Harbour Island dive. Its walls are layered with the covers of hundreds of record albums and sports posters that music-industry and basketball buffs find fascinating. The Vic-Hum is open 24 hours a day, catering to breakfasting construction workers in the morning, then locals meeting friends for a beer all afternoon. Some of them play basketball on an indoor court that is transformed later in the evening into a dance floor -- the music begins at 10pm every Friday and Saturday.

Snorkeling

Snorkeling Around Harbour Island

A small island off the coast of Eleuthera and measuring only one and half square miles in size, Harbour Island is to this day only accessible by boat. Unfortunately, not every boat has made the crossing successfully thanks to a ridge of very shallow coral reef. While this is bad news for the boat's captains, it certainly makes for some of the most interesting snorkeling opportunities in the whole of the Bahamas.

The Devil's Backbone is the name of this coral ridge, and here are dozens of bits and pieces of boats and their anchors that have been laid to rest here, then found themselves grown over with coral. Various small reef fish can be seen here in droves as well.

This isn't the only snorkeling draw around Harbour Island, however. This little island in the vast Caribbean Sea is also known for its blue holes and caverns. Several locals make their living offering snorkeling tours, but if you plan to go it alone, head to the east coast for all of the best sites. Some can even be accessed after a short swim from one of the pink sand beaches.

Snorkeling Sites

If you're ready to explore what's down below you might want to visit Man Island. This well secluded site is best known for its abundance of octopus which snorkelers have a great deal of fun interacting with. This snorkeling site is located on Eleuthera, North of Harbour Island.

The table directly below provides a few details regarding 3 of the best places where you can enjoy snorkeling in this area.

Snorkeling Sites Near Harbour Island

Site	Location	Island
Dunmore Town Bay	0.5 mi. Northwest of Central Dunmore Town	Harbour Island
Harbour Island	1.8 mi. North of Central Dunmore Town	Eleuthera
Man Island	3.1 mi. North of Central Dunmore Town	Eleuthera

Snorkeling Boat Trips

For some people, the best snorkeling is accessed away from the shore.

If you're hoping to snorkel during a boat trip, you can check with Valentines. While they call themselves a dive center, in truth, they offer every watersport you can image. Diving, snorkeling, fishing, kayaking, or a simple day of sailing can all be arranged and you can sometimes even do more than one a day.

You can look through the table just below for a list of the opportunity to take a boat ride that includes snorkeling.

Day Sails And Boat Trips On Harbour Island				
Name	Type	Phone	Location	Island
Valentines	Boating and Day-Sailing Provider	(242) 333-2080	Dunmore Town, Central Harbour Island	Harbour Island

There is a history to the underwater world that surrounds Harbour Island, making the snorkeling experience that much more important.

Attractions in Harbour Island

The small Harbour Island is as laid back a spot as they come. While there isn't much to offer by way of cultural attractions, the experiences you'll have mingling with locals as you relax on the beach, check out the small but satisfying dining scene, or simply stroll around town are worth forgoing countless trips to museums.

Beaches

You'll find a large selection of beaches to consider visiting on and near the island. Snorkeling is available at some locations, if some members of your party enjoy this relaxing pastime. You can click on the name of the beach for a detailed article concerning that particular stretch of sand.

Pink Sands Beach: Vacationers are sure to adore the pale pink sands of Pink Sands Beach which runs the entire length of the island's eastern side. The dazzling blue waters off of this coast are home to an amazing coral reef which protects this shoreline from dangerous wave breaks making this beach an excellent spot for casual swimming.

A second option that beach-goers can consider is Whale Point Beach. Tucked into the inside of a large cove, Whale Point Beach features some of the calmest ocean water you will find. Combined with the quiet area and the accessibility of the beach, Whale Point is nothing short of a tropical paradise.

Cistern Cay Beach: Cistern Cay Beach is a tropical paradise that has swimming access to another cay, albeit a very small one. Nonetheless, with the crystal clear water and abundance of rock formations, this area is active with coral, fish, and other marine life, making it a top snorkeling destination in the area.

Luckily, the area is home to a nice selection of beaches to choose from on and near the island. Make your way to this article if you're interested in learning additional details.

Historical Sites

If you enjoy experiencing the historical roots of foreign countries, you should consider visiting a historical site during your vacation.

A common landmark for vacationers is Harbour Island Haunted House. It is located within southern Harbour Island. According to legend, the mansion served as the home of a wealthy family until, one day, the family vanished in the 1940's. Over the years the mansion was left alone.

Take a moment to look through this table to read more about historic sites on Harbour Island.

Historic Sites On Harbour Island		
Name	Phone	Location
Albert Johnson Memorial	--	Dunmore Town, Central Harbour Island
Harbour Island Haunted House	--	0.8 mi. South of Central Dunmore Town

Caves

Even though most tourists are attracted by the beaches, those aren't the only way to enjoy the natural wonders available. Areas near Harbour Island some interesting options, including two caves.

You might want to visit Preacher's Cave, which is located on Eleuthera, Northwest of Harbour Island. Explorers beware, lest you suffer the same fate as

William Sayles; a captain who shipwrecked on Eleuthera in the 1600's and was forced to find refuge in what is known now as Preachers Cave. Today however, people seek out this cave for its natural beauty and wonderful photo opportunities.

The table directly below provides more details concerning caves.

Caves Near Harbour Island

Name	Type	Location
Hatchet Bay Caves	Cave	2.9 mi. Southeast of Central Gregory Town
Preacher's Cave	Cave	5.0 mi. North-Northwest of Central Mano Creek

Harbour Island Accomodation

As Harbour Island's only settlement, Dunmore Town features the highest concentration of all type of accommodations; however, as you move away from town you'll find that villas and rental properties become more readily available.

Hotels

You'll be able to find multiple types of hotels to select on the island, including a bed & breakfast and one resort. If you are hoping to stay active throughout your stay, you'll find at least a couple of choices that provide visitors with ample recreational possibilities. Click on the links to read further details.

Vacationers wanting to stay on Harbour Island should consider choices like Valentines Residences Resort & Marina. Valentines Residences Resort is located four miles from North Eleuthera Airport on Harbour Island, Bahamas. Set in the midst of pink sand beach and green flora, this modern-amenities hotel is for those looking for the ultimate in luxury pampering and relaxation. If you'd like to call before booking a room, you can do so at (866) 389-6864.

If you are wanting to book an accommodation with a lively late-night scene, Romora Bay Resort and Marina is one location you may want to consider. Romora Bay's junior suites and water view rooms offer guests spectacular views of the bay during the day and beautiful sunsets every evening. Each cozy room is equipped with soft down comforters, plush pillows, and even feather beds! If you want to call in advance, you can do so at (242) 333-2325.

If you're seeking to find a property with an active bar scene, Coral Sands Hotel is one destination you might want to think about. There is a wide array of available accommodations at Coral Sands Hotel, ranging from rooms and cottages to suites and a villa. There will certainly be a room to fit your stay and budget. Guests will be able to find them on Chapel Street.

Fortunately, there will be some other hotels. Go to Hotels page in this book for more information about more available hotels if you want to learn additional facts.

Condos and Villa Complexes On and Near Harbour Island

If you are not in the market for a standard hotel, you might want to consider renting a condo or villa in the vicinity.

Cambridge Villas is one property located in Gregory Town, Southeast of Harbour Island. Cambridge Villas makes for a great home base for vacationers who want to spend their days in the Bahamas exploring the islands. Free transportation is available from the villas to Golden Cays Beach, and there are a number of other beaches nearby, as well as various towns and cities worth exploring for their own special reasons. You will be able to find them on Main Street.

Be sure to look through this table for more information.

CONDO AND VILLA COMPLEXES ON HARBOUR ISLAND

Name	Phone Number	Star Rating	Location	Island
Cambridge Villas	--		0.0 mi. West of Central Gregory Town	Eleuthera
Chef Neff's Getaway	(301) 560-3166		Dunmore Town, Central Harbour Island	Harbour Island

Individual Villas/ Vacation Rentals, Homes & Villas

Some would rather have the seclusion offered by one of the many privately rented villas. Those wanting to get more information about the private rental properties on Harbour Island should read from villa rentals page.

Harbour Island offers a wide variety of vacation accommodations, ranging from ocean front cottages and bed and breakfasts to exquisite private rental houses, homes and villas. Locations vary from "bay side" to beach front, in town or on the outer ends of the island.

<u>Briland White House</u> - Only 101 feet from the shoreline and just 300 yards from the beach, a private dock, panoramic views over the bayside and the 'orangiest' of sunsets… This lovely new family home retains much of the unique Bahamian charm whilst providing modern living facilities such as central AC, back up generator, wifi and cable… a pretty cool pool too.

Infinity House - The ultimate beachfront vacation rental home on Harbour Island. This unique, four-bedroom, two bath home, along with guest house, sleeps ten comfortably. A 1,600 foot deck provides a breathtaking view of the pink sand beach and ocean. A one-room guest cottage sits next to the main house which has a king bed, toilet, sink and courtyard area with outdoor shower.

Hotels

Harbour Island Hotels
Advertising luxury rooms, beautiful views, and the best service imaginable, the hotels on Harbour Island are all well rated and even recommended. The type of vacation you're hoping for will inform your final decision. For example, someo hotels cater to active explorers, while others are designed specifically to provide a deserted island feel.

Hotels On Harbour Island

You'll be able to find multiple types of accommodations to consider on the island, including a bed & breakfast and one resort. If you are wanting to stay active during your stay, you'll find at least a couple of choices that offer travelers abundant recreational possibilities. Read more details regarding each of the properties by using the links.

Avid tennis players will like the idea of staying at Coral Sands Hotel. Rated by Caribbean Life Magazine as the "Best Small Resort in the Caribbean," Coral Sands Beach Resort is a quiet and peaceful escape on one of the world's most beautiful beaches. Recently renovated by renowned designers David Flint Wood and Barbara Hulaniki, the resort features a new British-Colonial style and luxuriously upgraded rooms and suites. You can find them on Chapel Street.

One destination along the oceanfront to consider is Pink Sands Resort. Pink Sands Hotel provides a unique Bahamian experience complete with a real pink sand beach. Guests will find themselves in a casual island atmosphere amidst lush gardens. You'll be able to find them on Chapel Street.

If you would rather book your stay at a top-notch accommodation, Rock House is probably a good spot to begin your search. There are 7 guest rooms and 3 suites to choose from at The Rock House. Each room features a king bed with a view of either the bay, garden, or pool. Visitors will find them on Bay & Hill Street.

The hotels on Harbour Island are simply some of the best in the Bahamas. Amenities vary and can include water sports, tennis, swimming pools, fishing, diving, boat rentals, and of course, fine restaurants. Weddings are easily accommodated at most hotels. Whether you're planning a family vacation or a romantic Bahamas getaway, Harbour Island has what you want.

<u>Valentines Resort & Marina</u> - Valentines Resort and Marina is legendary. When you think 'Briland', you think Valentines. It's a true upscale resort that attracts people of true taste and a love for life from all over the world. Boating and diving enthusiasts, yacht owners and families with a flair for the finer things in life... all find their way to Valentines. 242-333-2142 866-389-6864

<u>Runaway Hill Inn</u> - Historical 11 room beachfront mansion on Harbour Island originally built in the 1940s sits high on a hill of 13 lush tropical acres. Present owners have sought to maintain much of its original charm while adding sought-after comforts; Royal Trilogy Sealy Posturepedic beds with fine white linens, L'Occitane amenities,

reverse osmosis water purification system. A wonderful reprieve from hectic life. 242-333-2150

Also take a moment to look through the following table for more information about hotel options.

Hotels On Harbour Island

Name	Type	Phone Number	Star Rating	Location
Coral Sands Hotel	Hotel	(242) 333-2350		Dunmore Town, Central Harbour Island
Oceanview Club	B & B	(242) 333-2276		Dunmore Town, Central Harbour Island
Pink Sands Resort	Hotel	(242) 333-2030		Dunmore Town, Central Harbour Island
Rock House	Hotel	(242) 333-2053		Dunmore Town, Central Harbour Island
Romora Bay Resort and	Hotel	(242) 333-2325		Central Harbour Island

Marina				
Royal Palm Hotel	Hotel	(242) 333-2738		Dunmore Town, Central Harbour Island
Royal Palm Resort And Suites	Resort	(242) 352-3462		Dunmore Town, Central Harbour Island
Runaway Hill Inn	Hotel	(242) 333-2150		Dunmore Town, Central Harbour Island
The Dunmore	Cottages	(242) 333-2200		Dunmore Town, Central Harbour Island
The Landing	Guest house	(242) 333-2707		Dunmore Town, Central Harbour Island
Tingum Village	Guest house	(242) 333-2161		Dunmore Town, Central Harbour Island
Valentines Residences Resort & Marina	Hotel	(866) 389-6864		Dunmore Town, Central Harbour Island

Keep in mind, Harbour Island includes many other property types. To read more about other kinds of accommodations for Harbour Island, read from accommodation page.

Villa Rentals

Harbour Island Rental Villas

The main settlement on Harbour Island is called Dunmore Town for the once governor of the Bahamas who had a vacation home on the island. You too can experience the same joy he did during his off time by choosing to stay at a villa or rental property when you visit this quiet, natural stretch of land.

Individual Villas

You should have no problem finding a variety of standalone villas on Harbour Island. Many of them offer those who stay a unique style and variety.

The chart right below lists more details on the available rental properties.

Individual Villas On Harbour Island				
Name	Phone Number	Bedrooms	Bathrooms	Location
Afterthought Cottage	(203) 655-4286	4	3	Dunmore Town, Central Harbour Island
Apartment Royal	(242) 333-2788	3	2	Dunmore Town, Central Harbour Island
At Ease	(242) 558-3691	4	3	1.0 mi. South of Central Dunmore Town
Back Banyans Cottage	(242) 333-3805	3	2	0.8 mi. South of Central Dunmore Town

Harbour Island, Bahamas

Name	Phone			Location
Banyan Tree Estate	--	4	3	Dunmore Town, Central Harbour Island
Baybreeze	(615) 330-1209	3	3	1.0 mi. South of Central Dunmore Town
Beside The Point	--	5	4	Dunmore Town, Central Harbour Island
Beyond Reach	(242) 333-2278	4	3	Dunmore Town, Central Harbour Island
Blue Dolphin	(812) 339-8128	5	5	Dunmore Town, Central Harbour Island

Bougainvillea House	(202) 436-1492	4	3	Dunmore Town, Central Harbour Island
Breezy Hill	(242) 333-2241	4	3	Central Harbour Island
Briland White House	(242) 333-2278	3	--	Central Harbour Island
Buttonwood	(919) 932-3220	5	6	0.9 mi. South of Central Dunmore Town
Casa Triana	(242) 359-7074	5	3	1.0 mi. South of Central Dunmore Town
Chatterbox	(242) 333-2377	3	2	Dunmore Town, Central Harbour Island

Harbour Island, Bahamas

Ciboney	(917) 751-5979	3	3	1.1 mi. South of Central Dunmore Town
Coconut Ranch	(242) 333-3100	6	6	1.4 mi. North of Central Dunmore Town
Coconuts	(954) 636-5953	3	2	Dunmore Town, Central Harbour Island
Conch Pearl	(704) 644-2838	1	1	Dunmore Town, Central Harbour Island
Dunmore House	44 (0) 1666 503792	2	2	Central Harbour Island
Estrella	(713) 922-9055	4	4	0.7 mi. South of Central Dunmore

David Mills

				Town
FantaSea	(242) 333-2278	--	--	0.6 mi. North of Central Dunmore Town
Farcliff House	--	--	--	Dunmore Town, Central Harbour Island
Grapevine House	(843) 884-9801	3	3	Dunmore Town, Central Harbour Island
Gumelemi Bluff	(203) 618-3171	4	4	0.5 mi. North of Central Dunmore Town
Hibiscus Cottage	(242) 333-2278	2	3	0.9 mi. South of Central Dunmore Town

Harbour Island, Bahamas

Name	Phone	Bedrooms	Baths	Location
Hidden Mango	--	3	2	Dunmore Town, Central Harbour Island
Infinity House	--	4	2	Dunmore Town, Central Harbour Island
Juicy Hill House	(305) 972-3383	4	4	Central Harbour Island
Kismett Hill	(416) 471-3839	3	2	Dunmore Town, Central Harbour Island
Landfall	(242) 333-2278	4	4	0.9 mi. South of Central Dunmore Town
Little Arches House	(954) 336-4143	4	4	1.0 mi. South of Central

				Dunmore Town
Little Bay	--	4	3	0.6 mi. North of Central Dunmore Town
Mermaids Retreat	(242) 333-2582	2	2	Central Harbour Island
Oleander	(242) 333-3100	2	2	Dunmore Town, Central Harbour Island
Parrots Perch	(941) 364-9052	4	3	Central Harbour Island
Parrots Perch Cottage	(941) 364-9052	2	2	Central Harbour Island
Rainbow's End	(931) 260-6464	4	3	Dunmore Town, Central Harbour

Harbour Island, Bahamas

				Island
Salt Box	(242) 333-3100	2	2	Dunmore Town, Central Harbour Island
Sanderson house	(954) 253-1280	4	4	Central Harbour Island
Sandy Hill	(305) 205-3613	6	6	0.8 mi. South of Central Dunmore Town
Sea Dream House	--	--	--	0.3 mi. Northwest of Central Dunmore Town
Sea House	(242) 333-2278	5	5	Central Harbour Island
Seabiscuit Harbour Island	(401) 339-7489	3	2	0.9 mi. South of Central Dunmore

				Town
Seabreeze Sunset Harbour Estate	(242) 333-3100	4	4	Central Harbour Island
Six Shillings	--	--	--	Dunmore Town, Central Harbour Island
Solaqua	(717) 587-9675	5	3	Central Harbour Island
Still Point	(410) 925-2846	3	3	Dunmore Town, Central Harbour Island
Strawberry House	(447) 775-7529 ext. 31	3	3	Dunmore Town, Central Harbour Island
Swept Away	--	3	4	Dunmore Town,

Harbour Island, Bahamas

				Central Harbour Island
The Hideaway	(305) 205-4558	3	2	Dunmore Town, Central Harbour Island
The Kings Country	(954) 763-1527	2	2	Dunmore Town, Central Harbour Island
The Royall Lyme	(404) 915-3742	4	4	Dunmore Town, Central Harbour Island
Tree House	(310) 424-0200	5	5	Dunmore Town, Central Harbour Island
Tree Top	(242)	3	3	0.5 mi. North

	333-2278			of Central Dunmore Town
VRBO Listing #335471	--	4	4	Dunmore Town, Central Harbour Island
VRBO Listing #413451	(805) 637-8250	4	1	Dunmore Town, Central Harbour Island
VRBO Listing #472214	(242) 333-2278	5	--	Central Harbour Island
VRBO Listing #473071	(242) 333-2278	3	--	Central Harbour Island
Watercolor	(949) 466-0106	3	2	Dunmore Town, Central Harbour Island

Harbour Island, Bahamas

White Lodge	(212) 860-2332	5	5	Central Harbour Island
Yellowbird	--	5	5	Dunmore Town, Central Harbour Island

Fortunately, you can find additional property types to consider to choose from. Those interested can learn more about other kinds of accommodations available for Harbour Island read from Accommodation page.

Best hotels for short vacation or business trip

On the Graciosa Island, there are only three hotels and each of them attractive in their own way. For holidaymakers who got used to staying at the highest level hotels, the hotel Graciosa is the best choice. It is the largest and most popular hotel on the island. The hotel is located not far from the city center. A few minute walk and you find yourself on the beautiful beach, Porto da Barra. The hotel is ready to offer modern, fully equipped rooms for its guests. It is surrounded by lush thickets of exotic plants.

The hotel Graciosa has a beautiful panoramic swimming pool and state-of-the-modern gym. Its stylish restaurant serves many author's dishes and national delicacies. It should be highlighted that the hotel is suitable not only for relaxing vacation but also for work. The guests of the hotel can use equipped with modern technology meeting rooms and seminars. The hotel Graciosa suits all travelers.

The location of the residence Ilha is a completely restored historic mansion. There are 15 comfortable rooms for guests. One of the main attractive features of the hotel is the exquisite interior. Everywhere you can see the amazing decoration and furniture of light wood. Scenic residence will certainly be pleased for travelers who can't imagine a complete rest without sports activities.

There are tennis courts and a huge number of lovely locations for hiking and cycling. Those who expect to spend time in more exciting ways can arrange horseback riding with the help of the staff. For a relaxation, there is an extensive garden. Among the trees and flower beds, there is even attractive furniture for the garden.

The smallest and equally fabulous hotel on the island is Casa Das Faias. It is a lovely building which is close to the waterfront and popular beaches. The hotel can offer 8 comfortable equipped rooms for travelers. They are decorated with modern fashion trends. The Casa Das Faias hotel is ideal for vacationists who are planning to devote their leisure to beach activities and walks through scenic places. The staff can help you to organize leisure programs as cycling and fishing trips. Despite the fact that the selection of hotels on the island is quite modest here, tourists are provided with all conditions for an exciting holiday

Transportation

Harbour Island is semi-secluded and you will have to plan ahead to get there
Often ranked as one of the top vacation destinations in the Bahamas for its pink sand beaches, laid back atmosphere, and perfect watersports conditions year-round, Harbour Island is also a small and generally uncrowded island. A trip to this island will take some planning, but

those who have previously visited will surely assure it is worth the work.

Getting There

The majority of tourists who travel to Harbour Island get there by plane, but as the location has become more popular amongst millionaires and billionaires in recent years, yachting to the island has also grown in popularity.

Getting Around

Thanks to the small size of the island, vehicles are rarely necessary on Harbour Island. Most people can get around on foot, on a rented bicycle, or in a golf cart. There are estimates that there are somewhere between 800 and 3,000 golf carts on the island. Some tourists will rent golf carts for around $50(USD) a day, while others enjoy them as a perk of their vacation rental property.

Air Travel

There is no airport on Harbour Island. Instead tourists must fly into the North Eleuthera Airport (ELH) on Eleuthera, which is two miles west of Harbour Island. Like many airports in the Bahamas, this is a small facility with just one single runway, which is made of asphalt and measures 6,020 feet long. Regular flights to this airport arrive from Miami and Ft. Lauderdale in the U.S. State of Florida, as well as from the Lynden Pindling International Airport in Nassau on New Providence Island. The airport is served mainly by domestic and smaller commercial airlines like Silver Airways and it also welcomes chartered air crafts frequently. Learn more from Air Travel page.

Once you have arrived in North Eleuthera, it is just a 10 minute cab ride to the docks, which will cost you around $5, then another $5(USD) per person to take the water taxi to Harbour Island.

Sailing

While most will fly and then drive, sailing to Harbour Island is possible and growing in popularity. Not only for the wealthy with yachts, sailors from the US, as well as other Bahamian islands should have no issue setting sail to the island. As you might expect for any island of the Bahamas, the maritime activities here are enough to fill several vacations.

Ferries

Ferries are an important part of the transportation system in the Bahamas, and tourists can take advantage of this by island hopping during their vacation. The MV Daybreak III, a government run Mail Boat leaves from Potter's Cay on Wednesday at 6:00 p.m. and sails to North Eleuthera on a trip that takes just five hours which is short for a Mail Boat which are known for their slow movement. It costs $30(USD) for the trip, and when tourists arrive they can take the aforementioned water taxi from Eleuthera over to Harbour Island.

A vacation on Harbour Island is laid back and should be stress free, just as your planning should be. By reviewing the transportation options, you'll be better prepared to make your final decisions when that time comes.

Air Travel

If you plan to fly to Harbour Island, it will also be necessary to take a ferry
Direct air travel to Harbour Island is not a possibility, but you can get close enough to this destination by plane to still consider it a feasible option as you begin making your vacation plans.

Just two mile west of Harbour Island is the island of Eleuthera. This is the location of the nearest airport: the North Eleuthera Airport (ELH). It is a very small one, with just a single 6,020 foot asphalt runway, and a customs office in the building.

Regular flights are available from Florida, namely out of the airports in West Palm Beach and Ft. Lauderdale with Silver and United Airways. Another option is to fly to the Lynden Pindling International Airport on New Providence Island or Grand Bahama International Airport on Grand Bahama with an international carrier then switch to a domestic flight with BahamasAir or Sky Bahamas. Finally, you can schedule a charter from anywhere in the world if you're willing to pay a little extra for the private ride.

This chart indicates which airlines offer scheduled flights directly from the U.S. and the airports they fly from. The online booking services don't necessarily display the least costly options so it helps to realize which airlines provide direct service to this airport.

Governor's Harbour Airport U.S. Flights		
To/From	Airport Code	Airlines
Fort Lauderdale, FL, USA	FLL	Silver Airways, United Airlines

North Eleuthera Airport U.S. Flights		
To/From	Airport Code	Airlines
Fort Lauderdale, FL, USA	FLL	Silver Airways, United Airlines
West Palm Beach, FL, USA	PBI	Silver Airways

Flying to Harbour Island from the Caribbean

See below for a listing of scheduled air service from other airports in the region. If there are no flights from an airport near you, making a connection through a regional airport might be a very good solution.

Governor's Harbour Airport Caribbean Flights

To/From	Airport Code	Airlines
Freeport, Grand Bahama Island	FPO	Regional Air
New Providence Island, Bahamas	NAS	Bahamasair

North Eleuthera Airport Caribbean Flights

To/From	Airport Code	Airlines
Abaco, Bahamas	MHH	Abaco Air, SkyBahamas
Freeport, Grand Bahama Island	FPO	Regional Air, SkyBahamas
New Providence Island, Bahamas	NAS	Bahamasair, SkyBahamas

Next Stop, Harbour Island

The airport on Eleuthera is teeming with taxi drivers waiting to pick up tourists and deposit them at their accommodations. After making your way through customs, find a cab to take you to the docks. This will cost you about $5(USD), and from there, you'll be able to take the water taxi that travels to and from Harbour Island throughout the day. The water taxi costs $5(USD) per person.

There are a few different options to consider as you plan to fly to a vacation on Harbour Island. Make sure to review all of them to compare departure locations, scheduling, and cost which will help you to find the best flight for you in the end.

If you are contemplating an air charter, you can reserve one from the following regional agencies:

Charter Operators			
Name	Phone	Location	Island
Bahama Hoppers at ELH	(242) 355-1650	North Eleuthera Airport - Eleuthera	Eleuthera

Harbour Island, Bahamas

Flamingo Air Charter Service	(242) 377-0354	Lynden Pindling International Airport - 3.9 mi. (6.3 km) West-Southwest of Cable Beach	New Providence
Intercaribbean Airways at NAS	(855) 244-7940	Lynden Pindling International Airport - 4.1 mi. (6.6 km) South West of Cable Beach	New Providence
LeAir Charter Main Office	(242) 377-2356	Lynden Pindling International Airport - 4.1 mi. (6.6 km) South West of Cable Beach	New Providence
Pineapple Air at GHB	(242) 332-3811	Governor's Harbour Airport - 7.6 mi. (12.2 km) Northwest of Governors Harbour	Eleuthera
Pineapple Air at RSD	(242) 334-3000	Rock Sound International Airport - 1.6 mi. (2.6 km) Northwest of Rock Sound	Eleuthera
Regional Air Charter at ELL	(242) 355-	North Eleuthera Airport - Eleuthera	Eleuthera

	1720		

Ferries

Take the ferry or hire a private charter, and you'll be enjoy a leisurely sail to Harbour Island

There are no typical ferry services that offer direct trips to Harbour Island at this point in time; however, there are ways around it for those who need to make use to the sea as a source of transportation. One major ferry travels near enough to the island to let visitors take a water taxi the rest of the way, and the other is a private charter that those who are up for it can hire to take them on a tour.

Riding the Ferries

The best way to get to Harbour Island across the seat is to take one of the Mail Boats run by the government. The MV Daybreak III offers the service, leaving from Potter's Cay on Wednesday at 6:00 p.m., then sails to North Eleuthera. These boats are not known for moving swiftly, though, and it takes about five hours to get there. The trip costs $30(USD), then when you arrive you'll take the water taxi to Harbour Island.

In addition to the reliable Mail Boat options, Bahamas Ferries also offers a day trip to Harbour Island aboard one of their famous ferries. Although this isn't the same as using the ferry for transportation alone, it is an option for those who were considering island hoping to take into account. The service sails from the Bahamas Ferry ferry terminal to the dock in Spanish Wells on Eleuthera. From there, guests are treated to a tour of the island, and brought over to Harbour Island for an extensive tour of the island as well.

Make finding water transportation easy by browsing the selection of ferry services below.

Ferry Docks	
Name	Location
Harbour Island Ferry Terminal	Dunmore Town
Harbour Island Government Dock	Dunmore Town

If you're in need of inexpensive transportation or want to hire someone to take you on a tour with the added bonus of a quick jaunt across the sea, taking a local ferry is a great and reliable way to do so.

Ferry Routes, Harbour Island				
Location Served	Dock A	Dock B	Company	Frequency
Eleuthera	Harbour Island Ferry Terminal	Spanish Wells Ferry Dock	Bahamas Ferries	1 to 2 days per week

Harbour Island, Bahamas

| Nassau | Harbour Island Ferry Terminal | Bahamas Ferries Potters Cay Dock | Bahamas Ferries | 1 to 2 days per week |

Rental Cars

There is no need for a full-sized vehicle on Harbour Island

Rental cars are a go-to option for many tourists as they plan a vacation. They are so popular that when you book a getaway on-line, you can generally do so with a package that includes air fare, accommodations, and a rental car. Of course, it doesn't make sense to rent a full-sized vehicle for every destination you may be considering. Harbour Island is one of those places.

Renting a Cart

The small size of this island makes it so that renting a car simply is not necessary. You can walk pretty much everywhere you want to go, plus many hotel and rental home properties include the use of a non-motorized bicycle. If you much have a vehicle to get around, your best option will be to rent a golf cart.

There are somewhere between 800 and 3,000 golf carts on the island if you count those used by residents as well as tourists. They come in two and four seaters, are basically open to the elements, and though they move slower than a typical car, they are fast enough and powerful enough to get you around Harbour Island. In order to rent a golf cart here, you'll need to be over the age of 18 and in possession of a valid driver's license from your home country. If you intend to visit for more than three months, you'll need to apply for an International Driver's License.

Harbour Island, Bahamas

View the following table for several of the rental agencies located in this area.

Vehicle Rental Companies

Name	Phone	Location
Dunmore Rentals	(242) 333-2372	Bay and Church Streets - Dunmore Town
No Limits Rentals	(242) 333-2087	Upalong Road - Dunmore Town
Ross Garage Cart Rentals	(242) 333-2122	Harbour Island
Summer Boyz Golf Cart Rentals	(242) 551-3648	Johnsons Grocery Dunmore Street - Dunmore Town
Sunshine Cart Rentals Harbour Island	(242) 333-2509	Dunmore Town
Village Rentals	(242) 333-2161	Tingum Village - Dunmore Town

Rental Costs

The cost of a golf cart rental is somewhere around $50(USD) a day, though this can vary depending on how long you rent for, who you rent with, and the demand for rentals at the time you visit. Some accommodations include the use of a cart as part of their stay, so be sure to ask if this is true of your hotel or rental property before you reserve one elsewhere.

Gas Stations

A golf cart can be a fun and unique form of transportation. During your stay on Harbour Island you'll quickly become used to navigating the roads behind the wheel of one of these compact vehicles, and may like it so much you'll miss the convenience when you return home.

Sailing & Boating

On the edge of the Bahamas, Harbour Island provides for opportunities of fun
With the Atlantic on once side and the calmer Bahamas water on the other, Harbour Island is a

great place for sailors with an eclectic taste. Boaters will have the option to gently bob on the waters service, or to brace waves and currents. Fisherman will also have the option to angle for colorful tropical fish as well as hunt for deep sea game.

If you are just wanting to get out onto the water, without the complications and cost involved with renting a boat you can take an excursion. Wondering about this option? Take a look at the chart that follows to find contact information for area providers.

Boat Excursions

Name	Phone	Location	Island
Valentines	(242) 333-2080	Valentines Dive Center - Dunmore Town	Harbour Island

Docking

Harbour Island is an official port of entry, which means you won't have to make any more stops than absolutely necessary. As you sail into local waters, fly your yellow quarantine flag and put in a call to Harbour Control on VHF Radio Channel 16. A customs or immigrations official will meet you at the dock to review your paperwork and have everyone on board fill out immigration forms. At this time, only the captain will be allowed to leave the boat. Once the boat has gained clearance, and the $150 to $300(USD) fee for a cruising permit, fishing permit, and the departure fee has been paid, you're free to sail about the Bahamas for up to 90 days.

Harbour Island boasts two marinas, the Harbour Island Club & Marina and the Valentines Marina. Each has the necessary facilities to keep your boat running and your spirits high, including fuel, cleaning supplies, bathrooms with showers, restaurants, bars, shopping, hotel rooms, and more.

Are you going to travel to Harbour Island using your own boat, or a vessel you charter elsewhere? See the table that follows for basic information for nearby marinas.

Marinas

Name	Phone	Location
Harbour Island Club & Marina	(242) 333-2427	Harbour Island
Romora Bay Resort Marina	(242) 333-2325	Romora Bay Resort and Marina - Harbour Island
Valentines Marina	(866) 389-6864	Valentines Residences Resort & Marina - Dunmore Town

There are many memories to be made out on the waters surrounding Harbour Island. Whether you can sail yourself or need to hire someone to do the job for you, many agree there is no greater peace than bobbing along off the coast of a tropical paradise, enjoying the view, and simply sailing along.

Important Information

Pink Sands Beach is our favorite strand in all of The Bahamas; its sands stretch for 5 uninterrupted kilometers (3 miles). Although the beach is set against a backdrop of low-rise hotels and villas, it still feels tranquil and pristine. The sun is best in the morning (afternoons become shadowy), and the water is generally gentle, owing to an offshore reef that breaks waves coming in from the Atlantic. It has many good snorkeling spots and is also the island's best place for a long, leisurely morning stroll.

The diving in this part of The Bahamas is among the most diverse in the region. The most spectacular site, judged among the top 10 dives in the world, is Current Cut Dive, which is also one of the world's fastest (9 knots) drift dives. It involves descending into the water flow that races between the rock walls forming the underwater chasm between Eleuthera and Current Island. Swept up in the currents with schools of stingrays, mako sharks, and reef fish, divers are propelled 1km (2/3 mile) of underwater distance in less than 10 minutes. This dive may become one of the highlights of your entire life.

Valentines Dive Center, on the harborfront (tel. 242/333-2080; www.valentinesdive.com), offers a full range of dive activities. It's centered in a blue-painted wooden building near the entrance to the marina at the Valentines Resort. Lessons in snorkeling and scuba diving for beginners are given daily at 10am. Snorkeling trips cost $60 per half-day, including equipment. A two-tank 3-hour dive goes for $100, with night dives costing $105.

Lil' Shan's Watersports, Bay Street (tel. 242/422-9343; www.lswatersports.com), offers everything from scuba diving to boat rentals and fishing trips. A two-stop snorkeling jaunt goes for $65 per person, including gear. The staff here also offers special kids' programs.

Another worthy outfitter for exploring the watery depths around Harbour Island is Ocean Fox, Marina Road (tel. 877/252-3594 or 242/333-6300; www.oceanfox.com). A snorkeling expedition with two stops costs $65 per person, including gear, and two-tank dives are competitively priced with rates charged at Valentines .

If you're looking to rent a motorboat, try Michael's Cycles, Colebrook Street (tel. 242/333-2384 or 242/464-0994), near Sea Grapes nightclub. Plan to spend about $80 for a full day on a 4m (13-ft.) boat, or $110 to $185 for a full day on a 5m (21-ft.)

boat; rates do not include the gas charge. Kayaks go for $40 per day.

To book fishing guides and charters, you can either go through your hotel or contact the previously mentioned Valentines Dive Center (tel. 242/333-2080; www.valentinesdive.com), on the harbor side of the island in Dunmore Town.

My Harbour Island Personal Experience

fell madly in love with the rakish Sixties elegance of the Bahamas the first time I saw *Thunderball*. I was only a child yet imagined myself drinking Rum Dums while sitting at the bar of the wildly glamorous Lyford Cay Club in Nassau, dressed in Valentino and smoking Kent Lights, with a teenage approximation of Sean Connery by my side.

So when, in August 1992, an Argentinian fashion-editor friend invited me to go with her to the

Bahamas so she could visit a new lover, a local dive master she'd improbably met on a shoot, I accepted without hesitation. 'In August - are you sure?' people asked me, as if going during the hottest and most hurricane-prone season was somehow a mistake. It wasn't, it was perfect. And I quickly learnt we were not heading for the capital, Nassau, but to tiny Harbour Island (three miles long and half a mile wide, no bigger than a grain of sand on the map), a 15-minute flight away.

I remember the heat slapping me in the face as the pilot opened the prop-plane door upon landing in North Eleuthera, a neighbouring island with the area's only airstrip. But the breezy saltiness in the air immediately made me happy. I was young and felt as if I was finally meeting my exotic destiny. Our bags were collected and dumped in a taxi for a drive to a nearby cay that took approximately three minutes. We boarded a water taxi for another speedy ride to Harbour Island itself - an endless beach of the most unimaginably perfect coral-pink sand where the only mode of transport was (and still is) a golf buggy. That was 25 years ago. I've returned almost every year since.

Further south in the Caribbean there is chic French St Barth's, and even further again, almost touching Venezuela, aristocratic British Mustique - both magnets for tropical glamour hunters for more than half a century. Harbour Island, on the other hand, has been a slow burner, an insider's secret, lazily coming of age and stretching out its arms to visitors only recently, and still a little reluctantly. It's really only known by sailing and fishing enthusiasts, a few fashionable New York regulars who have been going for years, including Diane von Furstenberg, the Miller sisters, J Crew's Mickey Drexler and Revlon tycoon Ron Perelman. They've built houses that over time have grown to form sprawling family compounds along the Narrows. The most deserted part of the island, it can only be reached by bumping along a beautifully overgrown dirt track where hermit crabs and tortoises hog the road and shafts of sun knife through the wild canopies of bougainvillaea and hibiscus overhead.

This place might well have stayed a secret forever had it not been for Prince Charles's goddaughter, India Hicks, who came on holiday here, fell in love, but - unlike my friend - stayed with her British designer boyfriend, David Flint Wood, had four children and adopted another, opened a hotel (The Landing) and a shop, and is now Harbour Island's de facto social ambassador. She happily throws dinner parties around her pool for new visitors.

As often as I go, I am still hard-pressed to notice much change. I search the island's contours but the same pastel-coloured 19th-century colonial cottages I dream of ending my days in line the harbour-front like those on a vintage postcard. Valentines Marina, where boats moor (it's not deep enough for big yachts), has barely grown in the last 25 years. Although there is now an open-air restaurant and bar where crews discuss the weather while watching football and basketball games over hamburgers and bottles of local Kalik beer. But there are no Nikki Beaches or Nobus or waiting lists to get in anywhere.

Harbour Island can be confusing for those who arrive expecting to be instantly dazzled, because at first it feels indolent and quiet, not so much rundown as charmingly frayed and discreet. Where is the action? Locals go to church on Sundays dressed as if to meet the Queen; on weekdays children walk to school in immaculate uniforms, their hair in braids; in the early evening people chat on their front porches and play dominos, while at all hours roosters run wildly down the streets crowing. There are only two things that really count here: natural beauty and falling in with the laid-back rhythm. The 2,000 or so inhabitants will tell you how proud they are of the place they call Briland (the island's old name). Everyone you meet will want to chat, a sense of humour infecting their every word. My two favourite signposts for the local shop (it sells jam and books) read: 'Dilly Dally Dis Way' and 'Dilly Dally Dat Way', depending on which direction you're coming from. Agatha Christie would have adored it.

Until very recently, Harbour Island had few decent hotels. Pink Sands and Coral Sands, almost identical properties within yards of each other on the beach, have been here for years. Both are clean and friendly, and now a little spruced-up with private cottages, but, considering the prices they charge, not quite 21st-century enough and not always prepared for the cosmopolitan demands of their increasingly high-maintenance guests. I remember once staying at Coral Sands with a designer friend who on arrival to her room rang reception to ask where her mini-bar was and if someone could come and unpack her bags. The receptionist wasn't quite sure what she meant and the words 'island time' were spoken. She threatened to leave but somehow never did.

And then there was Pip's Place, further along the beach, more eccentric and full of character, with its giant open-air chess set and beautiful ramshackle cottages. It felt like an old antique shop and was where fashion photographers Peter Lindbergh and Gilles Bensimon stayed when they came for swimwear shoots.All the hotels have been tidied up, some more than others, although it's Pip's Place, now called Ocean View and run by Pip's son Ben Simmons and his Irish wife Charlie, that feels as if it could compete with an Ibiza-boho equivalent.

But no matter where you stay, at Ocean View, or in the new and very smart Bahama House in town, the main focus will always be Pink Sands beach, one of nature's greatest achievements. The sight of horses (they live just off the sand dunes) galloping through the surf makes my heart sing. However, Harbour Island is also confusingly more than just a beach. It might seem counter-intuitive but there's also something very special about Dunmore Town, as the two central streets are known, with all its kooky shops, restaurants and cafés (I say all, but there are really only a handful of each). It feels like the sort of village you want to know better, where you can imagine yourself living, and every year I am pulled between the two.

Harbour Island, Bahamas

We have rented cottages in town, and loved it, because you can sit on your porch eating breakfast while watching island life, and then later hear the fisherman laying out their catch on the dock. But this year I stayed at Ocean View, curious to see what the family handover had brought. Arriving here feels like stepping into a private villa; you go through the restaurant onto a terrace high above the beach, and then wind your way down paths passing one whimsical cottage after the next, no two identical, hoping each one might be yours. We were in the Boys Cottage, which Ben and his brother once occupied, the sea visible through the foliage, a little passage snaking its way to the sand below. At night, the waves seemed so close it was like sleeping on a boat.

The hotel has been dressed up with fashion photographs, a legacy of its glamorous past and present (Victoria's Secret shoots some of its swimwear catalogues on the island). Fabrics clash prettily with antique mirrors and quirky colourful china. Here island style is not about 24-hour room service, ironing and shoe- polishing, but charm and candlelit dinners on the terrace of barbecued ribs cooked by a young Haitian chef.

Then we did something unprecedented: we left Harbour Island. Ben also has a new project on North Eleuthera, an encampment of tents fittingly called The Other Side, which I couldn't resist seeing. After a seven-minute water-taxi ride from Valentines Marina we were deposited on a wild, deserted beach extended by a few feet with a stretch of lawn on which there are four massive, very photogenic safari tents. It's Robinson Crusoe, but with an Aman-style makeover.

The Other Side is small (it sleeps 12 in total, in three tents and three shacks further up on a promontory). Unless you want to stay marooned in your room, head to the drawing-room tent, with its backgammon boards and prints of Tintin on the walls, for cocktail hour when shakers are passed around between guests. Then it's on to the next tent a few steps away for dinner where you can't help but chat to new friends at the shared table. The bread is homemade and straight out of the oven, the main dishes are sophisticated and depend on whatever came in on the boat that morning.

Our high-ceilinged tent was lashed by rain and a fierce wind on one of the nights we stayed, but there was something so romantic about sleeping on a beach in such comfort while the weather roared around us. We awoke to one of those pristine Bahamian days where the sea is every colour of blue and green. For the adventurous, the hotel will organise expeditions down the long, thin snake of Eleuthera. The Other Side is a post to pitch up to when the excitement of Harbour Island gets a little frenzied, particularly at Christmas and Easter, and you can still pop over for dinner as it is so close.

But as ever we were excited to get back to the fray and try another recent opening - Bahama House, a small collection of colonial villas, shutters half open to the breeze, in the centre of Dunmore Town. We had driven past it many times without realising it was there. It is part of the Eleven Experience group, specialists in the very highest-end action holidays - places where you stay chic and you adventure chic, doing things such as kite-surfing on wild beaches or bone-fishing in secret coves. We rang a doorbell just off Dunmore Street, where a row of brand new golf buggies was parked outside in perfect formation. The New Orleans-style central courtyard is an oasis of one-storey houses, with a pool, sunken tropical bar, terraces and hidden alcoves shaded by tall palm trees. It reminded me a little of that James Bond Lyford Cay scene: old-world but elegantly modern too. We had our own concierge, and our first-floor suite - with expensive fabrics, a four-poster bed and complicated Lutron lighting - would have looked at home on the cover of an interior-design magazine. There is no restaurant but a chef arrives to cook breakfast to order on a terrace, and will return for dinner on request. The Bahama House was all anyone on the island could talk about during our stay.

While there we stuck to our ritual of an elevenses run to Bahamas Coffee Roasters for double macchiatos, burritos and cookies, followed by cinnamon rolls at Arthur's Bakery. We popped into Eva's Straw Work for locally woven bags, the Sand Dollar Shop for shells and India Hicks's designer boutique, The Sugar Mill Trading Company, for her immaculately tasteful gathering of homeware. Whenever we rent a cottage there are always mad dashes to the Piggly Wiggly or Captain Bob's mini markets before they sell out of avocados or bread. The Bahama House arranged a spot for us on the beach ('turn left at the bougainvillaea bush, just before the Narrows', we were instructed) with chairs, parasols and cold drinks.

They will organise a picnic too but my favourite lunch spot - apart from Coral and Pink Sands Hotels for fish tacos and beautiful terraces overlooking the ocean - has always been Sip Sip (the local word for gossip), a small restaurant up steep wooden stairs from the beach between Ocean View and The Dunmore hotel. You can't book but it's where the quiet billionaires, their guests and yachtsmen congregate to see who's newly arrived and who might be worth inviting for dinner. I always order a Goombay Smash cocktail and the conch-chilli soup; it's the ocean in a bowl.

The island explodes into life at night; people dress up (Lisa Marie Fernandez bikinis, Vita Kin kaftans, Zimmermann dresses and expensive straw bags bought in Saint-Tropez market) to flock to town for dinner. I particularly like The Landing, a hotel and restaurant set in an old colonial home overlooking the harbour. Elle Macpherson's ex, hedge funder Arki Busson, who has two houses on either side of the Narrows, adores it, as do Prince Pavlos and Princess Marie-Chantal of Greece. Both the service and food is good. Tables are laid out inside and around the fairy-lit garden, but pop into the wooden ship-like bar first for cocktails. (It also does a mean breakfast of ricotta pancakes and coconut bread.) Like Sip Sip, The Landing will give you the measure of the island. You do have to book and it isn't cheap. Or there is The Dunmore on the beach, which is a little more formal and less frenetic. The point is, like at lunchtime, there are choices and soon you'll find yourself on some kind of circuit, saying hello to people you saw only a few hours earlier eating conch fritters at the beach.

What happens after dinner is also important on Harbour Island. Open-air bars such as Beyond the Reef, Daddy D's and Vic-Hum crank up; graffiti covers the walls, table-tennis games get competitive, reggae and hip-hop blare out from massive speakers and the rum punches are volcanically strong. If you have teenagers, they'll be begging for curfews to be extended. And that's the thing about Harbour Island - you can come here as a child and before you know it your own children will be throwing you out of Daddy D's, bottles of Kalik hidden behind their backs, because they now think they own the place.

What Makes Sand Pink

Harbour Island is most renowned for its pale pink sand beaches some 3 plus miles long and 50 to 100 feet wide. The beach is considered one of the very best pink sand beaches in the world. The sand is a composition of bits of coral, broken shells, minute rocks and calcium carbonate from tiny marine invertebrates.

The pink color comes from tiny microscopic shelled animals known as Foraminifera. This animal has a bright pink or red shell full of holes through which it extends a footing, called "pseudopodia" which it uses to attach itself and feed.

These animals live on the underside of the reefs, on the sea floors, beneath rocks and in caves. They are washed up on shore as a result of waves or fish who knock them loose as they feed on them. Foraminifera are among the most abundant single cell organisms in the ocean and play a significant role in the environment.

Snorkeling and swimming are made safe and easy by the outlying reefs. These reefs provide large areas of relatively calm and shallow waters where the pink sand can accumulate in abundance.

Harbour Island Is So Tiny, It's Like a Neighborhood
Just a Crust of Land, But So Seductive, Says India Hicks

"Harbour Island is a crust of land only three miles long by half a mile wide. It is set off the coast of the bigger island of Eleuthera in the Bahamas' Out Islands."

"If you're looking for seclusion on Harbour Island, that's easy. But when you want a change of pace, you can have it. Harbour Island is easily reached by interisland flights and by ferry, including a high-speed boat to Nassau in the Bahamas."

Harbour Island Is a Welcoming Luxury Travel Destination

Weensy Harbour Island Will Win Your Heart, Says India Hicks

"As wee as it may be, Harbour Island makes visitors feel very at home. Welcomes are genuine and smiles are wide.

"There are several hotels and some pretty villas to rent here. My own home, Hibiscus Hill, has some cottages to rent. That is, when and if the invasions of family members leave!"

Harbour Island History Involves Both British & Americans

Harbour Island: On the Wrong Side of the Revolutionary War (Oh, Well)

"The Bahamas are now independent but were for centuries part of the British Empire," says India Hicks. "Harbour Island's history goes back even farther, when it was inhabited by indigenous tribes."

"In the age of exploration, the island was called Briland, and residents are still called Brilanders. They are very proud of their past. Since this is the Caribbean, of course that past includes sugarcane and rum. You can read island lore on Briland.com."

"As you walk past the bay, you will see the Loyalist Cottage, built in 1800. Loyalists were American colonists who sided with the British during the Revolutionary War era."

"As everyone knows, this was the losing side. The Loyalists were run out of the newborn United States. Some fled north to Atlantic Canada. Other Loyalists settled down in the Bahamas. Some ended up in Briland, surrounded by flowers and the aquamarine Caribbean. Not a bad way to lose a war!"

Harbour Island Is an Aquatic Playground
Harbour Island Is a Commotion on the Ocean

"You should spend at l east one afternoon on Harbour Island near, on, or in the water. You can take a swim off one of Harbour Islands' quite legendary pink sand beaches. The water is gentle and very warm. And the turquoise hue is unbelievable."

"You can rent snorkel equipment and wade right into the bay. Look for sand dollars and sea biscuits, but don't touch. Another aquatic activity: head down to Bottom Harbour to watch the turtles darting about. Keep a lookout for the family of dolphins who live here."

"You can take a spin with Captain Bob Griffin, who lives on the neighboring island of Current. Captain Bob will take you out on his boat to dive for conch or to spearfish whilst introducing you to a few friendly sharks."

"Or for a little more "depth," go scuba diving with Valentines Dive Center. (Their dive dock is shown above.) If you're not yet a certified diver, you can do a scuba "resort course" in the morning and be 30 feet into the deep by the afternoon! It is truly another world beneath the seas."

Harbour Island Things to Do for Landlubbers
India Hicks Says: Get on a Bike & Explore Harbour Island

"Not everything on Harbour Island involves getting your hair wet! Zipping around via golf cart is the mode of transport here no cars. You can **rent them** from our friend Sunshine. Or you can rent bicycles and cruise around at a leisurely pace."

"You can fall asleep under an umbrella on one of Harbour Island's quite legendary pink sand beaches. At the PLP dock, watch the fisherman bring in the day's catch. And right here on the dock, you can witness an aggressive game of dominoes, considered a national sport in the Bahamas."

Harbour Island Things to Do for Night Owls, According to India Hicks

India Hicks on After Dark on Harbour Island, in Her Words

"After the sun sets - spectacularly, I might add - there's nightlife on this bitty island. At night, you can wear your jeweled flip-flops to the Dunmore Beach Club for dinner, on the terrace, under the stars, the ocean before you and the tradewinds caressing you."

"And you can go dancing at Daddy O's into the wee hours if you have the energy. After a night of dancing, the most refreshing thing is a local Kalik Beer. I like to walk off a big meal by heading on foot up Gustie's Hill, which has marvelous views. The night sky, full of stars, and the midnight-blue sea below...it's almost too beautiful."

Harbour Island's Delicious Things to Eat
What and Where to Eat on Harbour Island

"Harbour Island has its own take on Bahamian food. It's very fresh and tasty, and served with flair.

"I like to go to Sybal's Bakery for local Bahamian breakfast of grits and stewed fish. Sunday Brunch could be at The Landing, where they serve ricotta pancakes and fresh-baked coconut bread."

"However, if you are feeling brave, Avery's offers the local dish of souse in all of these delightful flavors: chicken feet, pig feet, chicken, sheep tongue. This meat is what the local plantation workers ate, and they found ways to make it taste very nice."

"After a morning lying on the pink sand beach you will want to wander into Sip Sip for lunch. "Sip-sip" is the local term for gossip! And at Sip Sip you will indeed hear all the gossip, local and otherwise, and see anyone who's anyone. I recommend the Lobster Quesada and a Gombay Smash drink."

"The Queen Conch shack at the top of the PLP dock is a must for a late-afternoon snack. Here, local conch salad is made to order from local giant conch. The meat is pulled from its shell, chopped and mixed with the juice of limes and sour orange and local tomatoes, onions and green peppers. But beware: ask for 'tourist strength.' Anything else might blow your bikini off. If you are feeling adventurous, ask for the conch's *pistols*. Harbour Island men say, 'It puts lead in your pencil.'"

Harbour Island's One-of-a-Kind Shopping Opportunities
Harbour Island Tempts Shoppers

"For such a small place, Harbour Island has more than its fair share of sweet boutiques where you can find one-of-a-kind fashion and keepsakes."

"At the top of Gustie's Hill you will come across The Sand Dollar Shop. Here you can find many locally made treasures including little bottles of pink sand, which Harbour Island's beaches are renowned for. You might want to take one home to prove pink sand really does exist."

"I have a soft spot for The Sugar Mill Trading Co. It's my boutique. Here you will find an eclectic mix of treasures found from my travels around the world, everything from a $1,000 embellished evening caftan to a child's bucket and spade. The Sugar Mill also is the flagship store for India Hicks Fine Jewelry."

India's Harbour Island Residence, Hibiscus Hill
Hibiscus Hill Is India Hicks's Hearth and Home

India Hicks and her husband, David, own a magical Harbour Island inn called Hibiscus Hill. "The houses we have built are reflective of the wonderful, local West Indian style," says India. "Their bedrooms are cinematic lovers' retreats. Most rooms have large, wooden ceiling fans that purr as they gently ruffle the air. We conjured the rooms with images of old Bahamaian manor home in our minds."

"We have built or restored each house with fastidious care, and every one has its own personality. A lot of the furniture was handmade on-site by island carpenters. The house's living rooms open onto porches. They face the ocean or the toy-like village of Dunsmore Town, with its narrow streets and brightly painted frame cottages."

"Although they are guest houses, they have the feeling of a home filled with the gleanings of our travel and nomadic lives." These things include: "seashells from our scuba dives (all abandoned by their creatures first!); family photographs; native paintings from Cuba and Haiti; lacy mosquito nettings intricately woven in India; handmade bed linens; meticulously built model boats."

Harbour Island has often been called the Nantucket of the Caribbean and the prettiest of the Out Islands because of its powdery pink-sand beaches (3 miles' worth!) and its pastel-color clapboard houses with dormer windows, set among white picket fences, narrow lanes, cute shops, and tropical flowers.

The frequent parade of the fashionable and famous, and the chic small inns that accommodate them, have earned the island another name: the St. Bart's of the Bahamas. But residents have long called it Briland, their faster way of pronouncing "Harbour Island." These inhabitants include families who go back generations to the island's early settlement, as well as a growing number of celebrities, supermodels, and tycoons who feel that Briland is the perfect haven to bask in small-town charm against a stunning oceanscape. Some of the Bahamas' most handsome small hotels, each strikingly distinct, are tucked within the island's 2 square miles. At several, perched on a bluff above the shore, you can fall asleep with the windows open and listen to the waves lapping the beach. Take a walking tour of the narrow streets of Dunmore Town, named after the 18th-century royal governor of the Bahamas, Lord Dunmore, who built a summer home here and laid out the town, which served as the first capital of the Bahamas. It's the only town on

Harbour Island, and you can take in all its attractions during a 20-minute stroll.

The End

www.ingramcontent.com/pod-product-compliance
Lightning Source LLC
Chambersburg PA
CBHW031118080526
44587CB00011B/1018